Social Media Marketing 2017
Guide to Marketing Beyond the Search Engine

[KELVIN WANG DX]

Text Copyright © [KELVIN WANG DX]

All rights reserved. No part of this guide may be reproduced in any form without permission in writing from the publisher except in the case of brief quotations embodied in critical articles or reviews.

Legal & Disclaimer

The information contained in this book and its contents is not designed to replace or take the place of any form of medical or professional advice; and is not meant to replace the need for independent medical, financial, legal or other professional advice or services, as may be required. The content and information in this book has been provided for educational and entertainment purposes only.

The content and information contained in this book has been compiled from sources deemed reliable, and it is accurate to the best of the Author's knowledge, information and belief. However, the Author cannot guarantee its accuracy and validity and cannot be held liable for any errors and/or omissions. Further, changes are periodically made to this book as and when needed. Where appropriate and/or necessary, you must consult a professional (including but not limited to your doctor, attorney, financial advisor or such other professional advisor) before using any of the suggested remedies, techniques, or information in this book.

Upon using the contents and information contained in this book, you agree to hold harmless the Author from and against any damages, costs, and expenses, including any legal fees potentially resulting from the application of any of the information provided by this book. This disclaimer applies to any loss, damages or injury caused by the use and application, whether directly or indirectly, of any advice or information presented, whether for breach of contract, tort, negligence, personal injury, criminal intent, or under any other cause of action.

You agree to accept all risks of using the information presented inside this book.

You agree that by continuing to read this book, where appropriate and/or necessary, you shall consult a professional (including but not limited to your doctor, attorney, or financial advisor or such other advisor as needed) before using any of the suggested remedies, techniques, or information in this book.

Table of Contents

Contents

Introduction 4

Chapter 1 – Importance of Social Media Marketing 5

Chapter 2 – Reasons for A Failed Social Media Strategy and How to Fix it 8

Chapter 3 – Social Media Strategies for Boosting Brand Awareness 11

Chapter 4 – Key Elements for Social Media Marketing Plan 20

Chapter 5 – Optimization and Online Brand Development in Social Media Marketing 22

Conclusion 24

Also, Check Out This Other Book Published by Success Publishing 25

Free Bonus Preview 26

Introduction

Social Media Marketing is one of the most talked about words for anyone who is looking to improve their online sales and presences, but is SMM (Social Media Marketing) all it's cracked up to be?

A lot of SMM companies are springing up these days all over the place and they're telling everyone that they will completely listen about how important the social medias such as YouTube, Twitter, Facebook, etc. are important to your business, but for the small and medium-sized businesses, does social media marketing necessary? Is spending additional expenses to hiring an SMM company truly worth it? Also, has anyone made their research on this matter before deciding to hire someone to develop their Facebook business page? Some of the SMM companies set up online things like the Facebook business pages for $500 to $1000, which is in fact can be accessed and made for free by anyone, as well as telling their clients that they won't be needing to have a website because Facebook is the largest social networking site around the globe and nearly everyone has their own Facebook account. While it's true that Facebook is the biggest social networking site in the world, and Facebook members are all potential customers, it doesn't guarantee that they're really buying. SMM companies are all happy in pointing out the positives and benefits of social media like how many people are using Facebook or the total number of tweets that was sent out in the previous year, and the number of people that watch videos in YouTube every day, but are you really getting the complete picture?

In this eBook, you will get a good consider Social Media Marketing in regards to selling and knowing if it works, who did it work for and if it did, why did Social Media Marketing work for them? And should business rely so heavily on social networks improved sales and online presence as a marketing strategy beyond search engine.

Chapter 1 – Importance of Social Media Marketing

In the world of technology, communication has now become much easier than ever. Our working has now shrunk from a wide populated land to networks of communicating individuals existing in a global village. People from around the world have come much closer together and the distances have greatly decreased to the extent that every individual is just a click away.

This is what social media as well as the developments in the online communication can do. An event in one place of the world can instantly reach other parts of the world in a matter of seconds. Just imagine if that event or news was about your business or organization. This significance of this innovation is the ease and comfort it provides. By using this technology at your advantage can greatly provide you a lot of benefits which include the following:

- **Brings you much closer to millions of people around the world without too much effort** – Practically, SMM is free. If you plan to reach out millions of people manually through physical means, you would need to make lots of investments. SMM is the best way available to efficiently reach out your potential prospects, not just in terms of finances but also of time as well.

- **There are possibilities for discovery of new prospects** – As you review your viewers' feedback, you might start seeing obvious patterns in your business response. People from certain regions, which you might never have thought of show much interest in your product, are your best customers. You will also be allowed by to see particular untapped markets that you may exploit. You can move swiftly and make use of the opportunity.

- **Promote your services or products as serious business** – SMM provides you the access virtually worldwide and all potential clients. People are there to share and read anything that you need to say. This will become your chance to build an image for your business that you are serious about the services or products that you provide.

- **Making you more accessible** – Social media websites make sure that you will gain exposure 24/7. In line with this, your clients will be able to drop off a message easily and you will be able to select a reply as soon as you wish. This will help in strengthening the body between you and your customer, and thus, inspiring a feeling of loyalty for your brand. But you will not find this consistent availability when you deal with a physical office because of the office closing and opening times. This will be convenient for customers to reach out to you when they are in need and social media is the fastest way to reach out to one another.

- **Provides you feedback on type of viewers you have** – One of the most interesting things about SMM is the feedback level that you can get. As a matter of fact, through SMM you can get educated about the people who might be or are interested in your business services of products. This will provide you much better chances of changing your campaigns in order to gain much-improved results. You may also learn the number of people who are visiting your business page, or the ages of individuals who share or comment your posts, or event their localities, ethnicities, hobbies, religions, and preferences. You can get the world be aware of the existence of your product and services and at the same time educates you about the individuals who took great interest in it. You can get to know them much more through social media networks.

- **Your network is substantially growing** – The people who are added to your social network will become the cause for more people to join in. People that will keep adding the rate will grow with them. When the tree has branched out, your business will also grow.

- **More cost-effective and easier to manage** – Setting up a social media marketing campaign for brand awareness beyond the search engine will require you lesser effort as compared to when you plan to set out to traditional marketing campaign and execute your marketing campaign such as putting up advertisements, banners, and more, so as to get your message across. On the other hand, SMM is relatively easy to manage and frequently updated.

- **Your company will be seen as a person** – In general, most people do not prefer doing business with corporations or companies and they prefer working with individuals more. This is because a person is real, with a real presence in the world, someone whom you can relate to, and has thoughts, feelings, and emotions. Considering social media marketing for your brand will give it a human personification, and it will look more like an individual than a company, which is someone people can reach out to and can talk to, and thus, making a comfort zone between your company and the clients. It will then produce benefits for both of you.

- **Social media levels the playing field** – No matter if you are an individual startup or a multinational company, you will all be on the same level in the world of social media. Your resources and finances may not make any difference in terms of social media. But the different thing between one social media to another is the skill to attract and communication with people, as well as the quality of services or products that you are provided. On the other hand, startup companies face great financial difficulties to try promoting themselves, whereas the marketing of big corporations will continuously be dominating. Social media platforms will give you a fair playing field where you can show your skills and true spirit.

- **SMM brings worldwide popularity to your business name** – This will be your easy ticket to making an international level popularity. Your business or your name could become popular throughout the world with millions of fans and followers. Hundreds of millions of people can easily access social media sites where they come to express their views and communication online. Once you take advantage of the benefits of social media marketing, all of these individuals will instantly become your potential clients. Your business products or services will become a single search away.

Social media has been the new generation of information and communication transfer. Nearly all people keep visible of their online presence. You must not stay behind the competition and use this technology to your advantage.

Chapter 2 – Reasons for A Failed Social Media Strategy and How to Fix it

There has been an unbelievable reach of social media platforms and it has amazed entrepreneurs from all over the world. Both small and big businesses created accounts on social media sites and began to build a marketing strategy for various social media platforms. Nevertheless, while there are many partial methods to social media marketing, most businesses failed making a success to their marketing campaign. If you are among the business owners who failed connecting with the targeted audience and then engage them on social media platforms, introspection is the key. There are several reasons why your social media marketing (SMM) strategy failed and how you can fix it.

Failure to have understanding on customer behavior

Just as with any other marketing strategies, knowing your customers and how they behave is very important. A web designer or SEO will not be able to know the methods for building a marketing campaign on the social media by having an understanding about the customers' behavior. This why it is important to hire an SMM professional who can build a brand and making it famous among the targeted audiences.

Not having consistency

Even though you have a strong marketing plan with your first step being required to be a hit, if you do not have consistency with your social media marketing efforts, you will not have the capability to attain effective and long term results. It is among the greatest failures in SMM, and you can fix it by being committed to provide viral and engaging content across the year.

Putting the focus on your objectives and goals

Unlike the traditional methods of marketing, social media marketing is more about the wants of customers. Most social media marketers start their campaign by putting their focus on the business owner's goals. It would be a short-sighted approach to SMM because social media is not just about you. Thus, rather than focusing on you and your business goals, it is important to focus on the targeted market and their likes and dislikes.

Not working with the experts

SMM is not a joke or a job for children. Many companies assume that if they have accounts on Twitter, Facebook, and other social media platforms and as long as they put marketing messages and content on them, it would be more than enough to engage and connect with the audience. But it is far from the truth. There are lots of things that you should do to attain success on social media marketing. On the other hand, when you work with the experts, they will first do analysis on the market, conduct some research, and make proper strategies through assessment of the short term and long term implications.

Not listening or not considering the customer feedback and comments

It would be encouraging to see comments from the visitors on your posts. But if you cannot thank or follow up them for being interested in your brand, there will be a gap developed between you and your visitors. It is important to always make sure that there will be timely response provided to the feedback and comments of the visitors. 2-way communication is among the best advantages on social media sites and it must be used by marketers effectively.

Not spending enough money or time on social media marketing

Social media marketing is more affordable than the traditional marketing strategies, but it does not mean that there will be no investment to be done through money and time to attain the results you want. Rather than spending most of your marketing budget on traditional methods, it is great to consider putting in all your time and money on social media, because it is more effective, efficient, and more affordable. It is also reachable and will surely deliver visible results. To be able to get good returns on the time and money you invested, you should put in most of your marketing budget on SMM and get the performance monitored.

Relying on wrong performance metrics

It is another wrong approach is to measure the success of your SMM campaign on social media through the number of followers, likes, and fans. These are tricks that are only focused on increasing the numbers but it does not automatically get converted to customers. To be able to measure the success of the marketing campaign and your performance in a precise manner, you need to consider the elements that convert visitors like the number of retweets, shares, and more.

Not engaging users with your brand

Engaging with the users is essential in marketing. Engaging the customers with your brand is relatively easy, but there are still people who usually take it lightly and fail to engage the target audience with their brand. To be able to fix this up, the marketers must make sure that attractive, new, and engaging content will be posted on their social media profiles regularly. Making assessment on the marketing method of your competitors can also be helpful for you in coming up with effective methods to drive the traffic from your competitors to your own social media profiles.

So, next time you work on social media marketing strategies for your brand, it is important to be mindful of these mistakes to avoid them. There are several effective social media marketing strategies for boosting brand awareness through different social media platforms, including Twitter, Facebook, Instagram, and Snapchat. Read on to learn these strategies.

with the experts, they will first do analysis on the market, conduct some research, and make proper strategies through assessment of the short term and long term implications.

Not listening or not considering the customer feedback and comments

It would be encouraging to see comments from the visitors on your posts. But if you cannot thank or follow up them for being interested in your brand, there will be a gap developed between you and your visitors. It is important to always make sure that there will be timely response provided to the feedback and comments of the visitors. 2-way communication is among the best advantages on social media sites and it must be used by marketers effectively.

Not spending enough money or time on social media marketing

Social media marketing is more affordable than the traditional marketing strategies, but it does not mean that there will be no investment to be done through money and time to attain the results you want. Rather than spending most of your marketing budget on traditional methods, it is great to consider putting in all your time and money on social media, because it is more effective, efficient, and more affordable. It is also reachable and will surely deliver visible results. To be able to get good returns on the time and money you invested, you should put in most of your marketing budget on SMM and get the performance monitored.

Relying on wrong performance metrics

It is another wrong approach is to measure the success of your SMM campaign on social media through the number of followers, likes, and fans. These are tricks that are only focused on increasing the numbers but it does not automatically get converted to customers. To be able to measure the success of the marketing campaign and your performance in a precise manner, you need to consider the elements that convert visitors like the number of retweets, shares, and more.

Not engaging users with your brand

Engaging with the users is essential in marketing. Engaging the customers with your brand is relatively easy, but there are still people who usually take it lightly and fail to engage the target audience with their brand. To be able to fix this up, the marketers must make sure that attractive, new, and engaging content will be posted on their social media profiles regularly. Making assessment on the marketing method of your competitors can also be helpful for you in coming up with effective methods to drive the traffic from your competitors to your own social media profiles.

So, next time you work on social media marketing strategies for your brand, it is important to be mindful of these mistakes to avoid them. There are several effective social media marketing strategies for boosting brand awareness through different social media platforms, including Twitter, Facebook, Instagram, and Snapchat. Read on to learn these strategies.

Chapter 3 – Social Media Strategies for Boosting Brand Awareness

Social media is an important that may exponentially increase your brand's visibility within an arena in which many people simply get lost in the crowd. It may be difficult to know where you should start when it comes to using social media platforms like Twitter, Facebook, Instagram, and Snapchat to increase brand awareness. Social media marketing help raise your profile, so it is a must for businesses to have a strong online presence. However, with most companies getting ahead of you with their knowledge with different platforms, these social media marketing strategies will help boost brand awareness for you through Facebook, Twitter, Instagram, and Snapchat. Learn how each of these platforms leverage your brand to getting to the peak and beyond the search engine.

a. **Facebook**

   Facebook has still been the most valuable social media platform for online marketing. Because it has billions of active users, it is offering direct and unprecedented access to customers. Using this social media platform will require you to understand how Facebook works and how customers use this platform. As a major social media platform, you may face several challenges when trying to market your brand.

   Building brand awareness from the scratch

   All brands start out from scratch. It is essential to start building brand awareness by building a solid foundation. Put efforts to build a solid identity for your brand before moving into social media. As soon as you started using Facebook, you can now start reaching out to the community by targeting the demographics that have big possibility to use your products and/or services.

   You may view people who follow your competitors, those who are quite interested in the same product or those who are in your geographic location. Your brand will certainly grow if you made a solid foundation and care for this foundation well. Building initial brand awareness on Facebook will take great amount of time, and necessitates momentum. If you stop building your brand, you may find yourself losing steam. Because of this, you must have a good idea about where you will go and how you will be able to get there from the scratch.

   The use of incentives for increasing brand awareness

One way to increase brand awareness through Facebook is by using incentives. It can increase your presence in Facebook by 40%, because the nature of Facebook is for customers to share information. With attached incentives to your social media marketing campaign, you are leading the customers to feel like they are sharing something valuable. Incentives will depend on the involved company, such as free shipping, trials or samples, and discount coupons, among others, are all examples of valuable incentives that are most commonly shared.

To use incentives in a proper way, you will have to determine a low-cost offer to be provided to customers, which may be compelling to new customers. Nevertheless, you should also keep in mind that you should already have a strong brand identity when you offer incentives. You would also have to be ready for the incentives. You may experience a great traffic influx when the incentives really take off.

Running contests instead of straight promotions and marketing

Contests have its own way of driving people wild. As compared to incentives, which is quite costly, a contest often enables you to control the money to put out. When you create a contest like a simple free coffee for one year, you can gain a customer base. You only need to put in the initial work to get your contests out there, and the customers will instantly start to participate. You can even get more success in contests if you ask those who are signing up for the contest to refer friends to get more entries or as one of the requirement to join. This kind of promotion has high possibility of growing quickly, more particularly through a social media platform that is accessible and active like Facebook. Contests may not always lead to instant dollars, but it can improve your brand identity and increase brand exposure.

Keeping an eye on your statistics

It is essential to keep tabs of which social media marketing strategies through Facebook are doing well and which are not. You would want to put emphasis on the content to be shared. About 70% of customers trust a brand recommendation from friends, and there would only be 10% of prospects who would want to trust those that purely come from advertisements. Because of this, you need to focus on quality of the content you will share. But it is not always possible to know which content will become more famous.

The web may be a complicated place, so one of the best ways to determine the best campaigns is by keeping an eye on your statistics. In line with this, you can figure out which will work best for you and your brand. You may feel like you are trying lots of different things but you still do not get significant results in the beginning but you will see that you are developing a feel for the contents that will be famous.

Engaging with audience

Facebook really shines in the capability of engaging your audience regularly. With SMM through Facebook, you can speak to your prospects or current customers directly regarding the issues that matter to them. One important thing in general SMM, particularly in Facebook, is never neglecting this component. Most brands are receiving positive comments when they speak with their customers candidly and openly with regards to their products and services. There is nothing better than having positive comments and feedbacks for building a brand identity.

In addition, you may also consider studying your customers to see what they say about your brand on Facebook. This will offer unique capability for gathering information about what factors would add attraction to your brand and which of your Facebook SMM strategies work. It can even give you several insights to varying directions that you can take with your social media campaign.

While Facebook is the most popular social media platform these days, it is not the only important thing. A comprehensive brand awareness campaign will require different platforms working together to be able to make a targeted and cohesive strategy like Instagram.

b. **Instagram**

If you want to get your brand and products seen by more and more people, growing a strong following who relate to your brand is your magic spell. Instagram has now hundreds of millions of monthly users, which is more than Twitter, and so lots of brands find ways to interact with Instagram community and can earn invested customers to keep coming back for more in their offerings. However, it is not only the numbers that you must care about, but the people who are using this platform.

Instagram users are shoppers. About 70% of Instagram users have been reported to looking up a brand. If you post the right Instagram photos, customers will soak up your marketing message without any difficult sales pitches from you, and thereby, you can leverage from your magic spell to appeal to customers without a need to sell to them. If you are new to IG, no need to worry because all things you must know for marketing your brand is covered here. There are also more advanced tips for you.

Setting up your optimized business Instagram account

When making an account in Instagram, your business account needs to be separate from your personal account. Remember that social media marketing (SMM) is all about the audience and not about you, so keep all your snapshots and selfies from your travels with your loved one to remain personal. They do not have any relevance to your customers and it will not increase your sales.

As a matter of fact, your image should rarely appear in the IG page of your business, or not at all. The important things to include in your business account on IG are a link that will boost traffic to your website, interesting and informative Bio that will hook followers, and staying recognizable with a consistent photo and name. Hashtags and keywords will not really matter because they cannot be searched when they are on the bio. You will always be able to change your bio for the promotion of your latest sales, campaign, or launching, but do not ever forget a link.

Creating famous IG posts that other users would certain want to follow

A picture indeed is worth a thousand words, so leverage from the full power of hooking customers to your advantage through a photo. The increasing popularity of Instagram with its photo-centric platform gets 2x as many comments on posts that have image as compared to posts in other social media platforms that post just links or text.

One thing to keep in mind is avoiding hard selling to appeal to the social culture of IG. Photos enable viewers to make their own decisions without feeling pressure from the business, and remove the salesman aura from the scene. It is also advisable to promote your products and services with professional and creative photos. The power of product images was always important to shopping online, and the visual platform of IG is taking that power to the next level. IG is a social marketplace that can direct traffic into sales. It works by sharing photos that are unique, attention-grabbing, and full of personality.

Prioritizing professional quality

Do not post blurred or crop images because it can reduce your professionalism points. The format of Instagram makes your images automatically square. In line with this, consider the square shape when you select an image, or the entire appeal of the photo may be lost. Be sure your images will reflect professionalism, which requires you to post only high-quality images. A safe estimate to preserve the quality is by saving your photos at double resolution size.

Making unique lifestyle images that can capture your brand culture

Because your business Instagram account is not a direct sales market, you must put your focus on adding appeal and value to your news feed if you want to retain your followers and have more. The best party trick to inject your Instagram feed with appeal is through lifestyle images. You may use life-inspired scenes, backgrounds, and models to add a scene in your product. With this, users will most likely to image how great those products would look when they wear them out on a certain occasion.

In the marketing terms, do not present only the products and services that you offer, but also the lifestyle and culture that surround them to strengthen your brand equity. It would be the associated feelings with the brand. You may also post some suggestions on how to use or wear the products of your offering.

Offering exclusive announcements and promotions to followers

Just like Facebook, you should also pump your followers up with special offers, bonuses, and insider announcements on their feeds. Because more than 40% of IG users state that they follow or will be following a brand to take advantages of giveaways and benefits, it will give them that incentives. You can make use of text overlay so that you can include your promotion right on the image, and it has also been a visual and stylish way of announcing discounts and sales.

Reaching a wider IG following

Even if you have been posting amazing images, it is also important to have an Instagram social media marketing strategy to get people to start following you. You may include hashtags to increase your discoverability. You can also invite IG ambassadors to share your brand. Create a team of ambassadors who will spread the advantages of your brand to all their own followers. Encourage your followers to post reviews and photos to reach more users.

Another way to reach a wider Instagram following is by sharing the tagged photos on your own profile. It is a social media marketing bonus for you, which will save you lots of time because it basically hands over excellent images with just the tap of a screen.

Boosting customer engagement on Instagram

If an Instagram image has been shared and grew followers, but how will you be able to solidify that following into paying and loyal customers? It is through customer engagement. By closing the gap in communication between seller and buyer, IG is offering the chance to enhance your customer services, as well as receive any direct feedback from your customers, and even build relationships that may lead the visitors into loyal customers.

Keep in mind that the social nature of Instagram is to increase the more intangible aspects of social media marketing, such as brand equity, buyer loyalty, and lifetime user value. The associations and community of your brand are just as essential as your products and services, and IG is a platform that helps in promoting brand identity. Customers will soon come to you.

c. **Snapchat**

From 2015 to 2016, the monthly active users in Snapchat have doubled from a hundred million to 200 million of active users. It has shown essentially faster growth as compared to Twitter, Instagram, and Facebook. It has come a long way since its inception in year 2011 with its imaging sharing social media feature. Snapchat is among the best places for growing business. All you need is to know how to do it.

Everyday snaps to increase product and business knowledge

While it has a smaller impact on the bottom line of your business, it can do a great deal for you, more particularly if you are just getting started or if you have a unique product. Having daily snaps will help putting cement on your business within the top-of-mind awareness of your followers. They can also increase your Snapchat's value because followers want to see more than just a collection of carefully taken discount codes and product shots.

Several ideas for the daily content on Snapchat are videos highlighting the culture of your business, behind-the-scenes images, or Snaps that show different ways to use your products or several features. Take advantage of the drawing tools and filters for crafting engaging and creative snaps.

Consistently posting will help you inform your followers of various products, providing more familiarity with your business. This can increase the possibility of turning them into sales and loyal customers in the future.

Snapchat-exclusive promotions for increasing e-commerce sales

Promotions on snapchat rely on your business that has already growing Snapchat following. The more followers you have, the more possible customers you can reach. Aside from your everyday snaps, you may include occasional codes and discounts. The main purpose of this strategy is by converting your followers into sales. But it also serves a long-term and secondary purpose. You will be able to advertise Snapchat discounts on your other social media accounts to be able to grow your list of followers on Snapchat.

Q & A on Snapchat to create meaningful relationships with followers

Even though it may seem hard, hosting a Q & A on Snapchat is one great way of taking an established Snapchat following and be converted into sales. You can set a time and date to host your Q & A and then encourage your followers to send in questions and on your other social media platforms. Snapchat videos are good for this. Allowing advanced question submission will ensure that you would not have a shortage of questions when you finally air your Q & A.

If you got too many questions, just choose the best or the most appropriate among all the questions, but keep in mind that not all questions should be related to your product or business. Keep some less serious questions as a chance to show off your personality. Read out the question and shout out the author when you answer. This will make them feel recognized and thus, creating a personal connection to your brand.

These are just few but very effective tips to grow your business in social media marketing through Snapchat. Learn more tips on Twitter SMM.

d. **Twitter**

Twitter is another very effective tool to increase brand awareness. It helped lots of people in growing their business. With more than a hundred million people on the social network each day, it has been among the major social media marketing platform for business success. There are several things that you need to keep in mind to become successful in social media marketing through Twitter.

Picking the right times

Your customers have a time when using Twitter. Test out various times to figure out when they use Twitter. One good sign that your audience is most available is when your posts gets comments, likes, and retweets. You may also check your competitors and see when they usually post and how much engagement they are receiving on various kinds of posts during different times of the day.

Finding your keywords

To leverage from social media marketing through Twitter and promote your brand successfully, you should master the art of using and finding the right keywords. Keywords are ultimately important to SMM, because they can help increase your tweets' popularity by making your posts easier to categorize and find.

All the better news is that you will be able to conduct the right keywords and key phrases through simple search from your Twitter account. For instance, when you search for writing job, you may also find other keywords like freelance writing, writer, freelance jobs, content writing, content writer, blogger, and more. Be sure to keep a list of the best keywords for your business and you should use them for creating buzz around your brand.

Being consistent

No matter if you have great content to share with your followers, have a professional Twitter account, and/or a quality product that you can pitch, you will not succeed in your social media marketing campaign if you are not consistent. Do not tweet every 2 days or once a week. You should tweet each day. The goal of using Twitter is by engaging quality content with your audience, which has relevance to your brand and which adds value to the lives of your followers, helping your audience like, know, and trust you. You will only be able to do this when you are present in their online lives.

Harnessing hashtags

Hashtags are used for marketing topics or keywords in a tweet. With a hashtag, you are categorizing your tweet so that people can easily found it, and this does not only make it simpler for people to find your tweets, but you will also be able to improve follower engagement. You can use popular and current hashtags. You can also create your own or jump on other Twitter users' bandwagon and use a trending tag to attract people to your posts.

Selecting a catchy name

Choose a professional name that your followers and prospects can remember and relate to. It should be a name that is irresistible that Twitter people cannot help but follow. You should keep it relevant and it is important to include at least some parts of your business name. It can be the abbreviated version or other things that come to your mind. But keep it short.

Chapter 4 – Key Elements for Social Media Marketing Plan

As with any business marketing strategies, you need to have a plan for success and utilizing social media is no different. For you to effectively use social media as one viable business marketing strategy, you need to have a secured plan in place. Just as having a business marketing plan, you need to have a marketing plan for utilizing social media. Therefore, when you're writing a plan to get social, you must consider the most important element to ensure your business success. After all, there is nothing worse than wasting both your time and efforts on something that is simply not useful or beneficial for your business. Social media is now considered as one of the most effective tool for businesses when used in the right way.

Here are the top 5 most important elements you need to consider in your social media business marketing plan:

1. **Business Objective** – First and foremost, you need to figure out what's your overall goal to using many different communication channels online. You can use the social media platforms to build your brand online, sell a service or a product, or get to interact without the customer base. No matter what you goal is, your content should be aligned with your objectives. Your main reason for being in the business is to effectively address a problem or solve it held by a specific number or group of people, for example, you target audience. Therefore, your online strategy should also tackle the needs and wants of your target audience.

2. **Media Outlets to Utilize** – There are a lot of online platforms to choose from. However, it's very important to know which of the social media platforms are best for your business as well as for your target demographic. Identifying which platform to use is a primary source of the contemplation for a lot of small business owners. One of the best ways to get a clear understanding of what social media platform to use for your business, you need to figure out where your potential clients and prospects hang out. The easiest way to achieve this is by having a survey that simply asks your followers about the top 3 social media websites that they use. It's much easier to have this kind of information upfront than spending your time in using the social media platform where you will get just a few following or engagement.

3. **Engaging Content** – Have you ever heard of the saying that "content is king"? This also applies to using social media sites as well. Your content needs to be educated and can inspire a response and a reaction. It's crucial to provide the necessary information to your audiences in a compelling and unique way. Of course, regardless of what industry you are in, there are hundreds and thousands of people sharing the same information on similar subject, that's why you need to identify a way to stand out as well as make your content unique and unforgettable.

4. **Customer Policy** – Customer service can make or break the reputation of your company. Your customers should get a feeling that they are valuable to your business for them to continue buying your services or products. It's also the same with using social media; your followers should get the feeling that you are completely willing to provide help and assistance about their needs. Using social media sites for marketing should include a plan on how you will handle your customer complaints and concerns online. In addition to that, you need to assign someone who will be responsible for the entire online communications of your business and have the know-how about getting engaged with current customers as well as with potential customers.

5. **A System for Measuring Outcomes** – When it gets right to it, success should be measured for your business to grow. Your social media plan needs to include certain types of metric to gauge the effectiveness as it relates to your entire online objective and goals. You need to identify how well you've achieved the first things you set to do. Were your goals to achieve a certain amount of sets every quarter or each month met? Did you utilize new sales tactic or promotion? How well did they work? Were your goals to achieve a certain number of fans or followers met? Did you meet your goals or fall short? Based on how well you meet your goals, you need to provide you company a grading in order determine the room for improvement. Having the measuring system for outcomes will help you in determining how well or effective your plans are.

Social media is without a doubt a viable tool for marketing but needs not to be the only marketing strategy you will use if you desire having a sustainable business growth. To make your business achieve success, you need to plan your social media business marketing just as your do with anything else.

If you don't have a plan about how to use online networks, you should make one based on the business objectives you desire you company to achieve online. If you have a marketing plan, just review it carefully for effectiveness.

Chapter 5 – Optimization and Online Brand Development in Social Media Marketing

Online marketing has never been as easy as we expect it to be, more particularly in terms of branding and working within a budget. In this case, you must pay attention to all details and resources about how you would market your online business. The wrong processes will lead to wasting money and time, and outstanding online marketing strategies will provide increase conversions and online exposure. Social media marketing became a famous alternative for online business branding. Companies are not thinking of social media sites as websites for children. They are now valuable networking and online marketing resources for business.

Getting started

Before you get started in SMM, you must nip the urge of joining each social media platform. It is not hurtful to have online presence everywhere, but there is not advantage in wasting time when you set up a social media account that is not active. The website owner may delete it or it may have been outdated and looked unprofessional. Also, there is no way to work them unless you have some help. You should also have a plan of action to be able to position your company correctly from the start.

Proper setup

It is important to learn how to setup and position your company with the best social media marketing platforms like Facebook, Twitter, Instagram, and Snapchat. Among the significant initial positioning details that you consider, including selecting the right username for your profile links, identifying which are the best social media marketing platforms for your interests and niche, selecting the most attractive media and profile information to share, establishing a time schedule that permits working as many networks as possible, developing a skill for some filtering activity in accordance to the appropriate social media site, and more.

Implementing

A predefined SMO strategy should be include, expediting the professional results that you need for your business. It is easy to assume that social media marketing is just setting up social media networks and marketing, but while it is a part of the process, social networking is not involved in SMM. The key to this offsite marketing process is content, like articles, discussions, videos, blogs, images, link, and other things that social media marketing needs to correspond with the SEO.

Social networking and online brand development may seem easy but it is not a simple process. There are defined strategies that must include both social media marketing and search engine optimization to be able to build a process called social media optimization. Generating social media marketing will help you learn how to brand your business online properly and lead your business to sure success in the social media.

Conclusion

Are you tired of spending many hours on social media and do not know if it is working? This guide helps online marketers to learn more about leveraging the power of social media marketing. A business will almost not be able to survive in the world without online marketing. The best thing about it is that social media marketing is effective, cost-effective, and can work for anyone.

Any businesses, not matter how small or big, will be able to market its brand online through social media marketing. Make sure to have a comprehensive social media marketing plan before starting to consider how every social media platform among Facebook, Twitter, Snapchat, and Instagram, can enhance your business, and you would not go far wrong.

-- Kelvin Wang DX

Also, Check Out This Other Book Published by Success Publishing

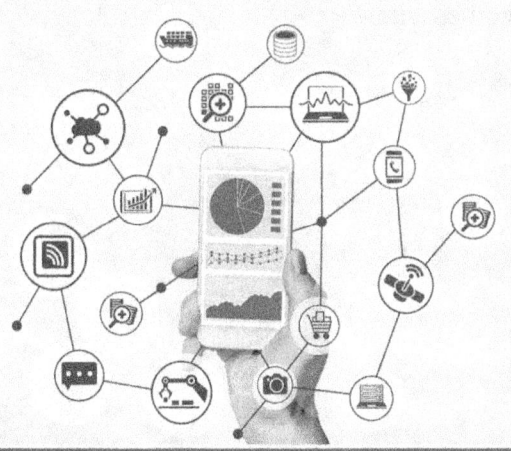

Automatic Income Machines

Free Bonus Preview

Automatic Income Machines: e-Business Blueprint

With an economic whiplash that hits most the countries today; more people are joining ranks in achieving economic progress through the internet. The internet world had become an American Dream while others look at it as the other side of the world with the greener pasture.

Many had indeed taken their chance in starting an online business, yet not all are ready to face all the challenges and the complexities of surviving in the internet business arena.

However, for those who were lucky enough to survive, they lived to testify to the kind of life online business offers.

This "e-Business Blueprint" aims to provide beginners with a guide on setting up an online business and guiding you through the simple steps to achieve success.

With proper knowledge and determination, success on any online business can be achievable and in fact, rewarding. It's just a matter of planning and driving you towards a goal that can really make your dream comes true.

CHAPTER 1: Reasons for Getting Into an Online Business

People got different reasons for going into online business. But most often, online business is for people who got tired of working 8-5 or 9-6 every day. Rushing each morning for a gulp of coffee before fighting his way through traffic and hoping he could be earlier than usual!

As you realized that you are getting tired of working for someone else and you want to become your own boss, you start thinking of the possibility to make it big in the internet business. Hoping, you are right, and then the best way to set up a business with a greater chance to make it to success is to start now!

Here are just a few of the many reasons why you must start with your internet business.

Goodbye to Traffic and Early Morning Rush

With an internet business, you don't need to rush up too early that you need to skip eating breakfast just so you can arrive in time for work. But when you are living in an overcrowded metropolis where you had to go through jam-packed traffic, stress and anxiety can be a daily part of your routine!

Online business can help you save a lot of money by not traveling every day. Count the savings you can have when you don't need to go out for work. You can likewise save your time and convert the time spent for daily trips into more productive inputs.

No Need Putting Up with a Toxic Boss

Most often people got fed up and want to get out of their work because they have a toxic person for a boss. Most often, bosses thought that their employees are there to please them all the time. This often happens when you are working in a sole proprietorship type of business or a one-man organization. Most often than not, you feed to your boss whims and schemes rather than get productive in your tasks. In the end, you feel thoroughly burnt out and find a quick way to change job.

Working at your own Pace and Time

When you are running an online business, you can be your own boss. You can work at a chosen time and place. You can even have more time to yourself and to your family. However, this can have its own drawback. So, before you get out of your work, be sure your finances or the lack of will not cripple you. Proper timing is needed so your family will not suffer from your decision.

When you are free to decide for yourself whether you are going to work or not, be sure you manage your time effectively and efficiently. When you're alone to manage your time and no one is around to put pressure on you, you don't give yourself a reason to procrastinate. You need to learn to balance everything even without someone to answer to. Remember that every minute wasted is an opportunity lost in online business.

Unlimited Income Potential

Working on a regular career means putting up a cap on how much you can earn. But with online business, your ability to earn depends on how much time you want to put into your business. You can earn as much or as little as you want. The market for online business is too vast. You just learn to tap its unlimited resources and you go as far as you can.

You can target people around the world as the global market is getting bigger and bigger and more people are learning how to access the internet every day. You can work as much or as little as you choose. The marketplace for internet businesses is worldwide.

Per the later report of the Statistics portal, the number of internet users had risen up to 3.17 billion this year from 2.94 of the previous year. Doesn't that market large enough to dip your toes into?

Minimal Expenses for an Office

Since you are working from the comfort of your home, you don't need to rent an office space. You will again be saving a lot on your administrative expenses compared if you are running a conventional type of business.

In setting up your business, all you need to have is your laptop or PC and low-cost hardware and software which you can even get for free online if you're just diligent enough to browse through your internet.

Bigger Chance to Achieve more for Less Work

An online business allows you to work fewer hours and achieve more. There are some business models that can be fully automated. You just must set them up and (lo!), they can run on their own and earns you a passive income. This automation process now is widely used in the internet market. If you can't run your business on 100% automation, you can at least have it automated at 50% or more, so you can have more time for additional business to carry on.

What makes an online business unique than conventional ones is you can operate multiple businesses single-handedly. To simplify, you are operating a business that is almost next to impossible – Less capital, less time, and less effort for unlimited income streams potentials.

Common Problems you will Encounter at the Start of your Online Business

Starting your online business can be both rewarding and stimulating. However, you are sure to encounter a few problems that new entrepreneurs usually encounter. To steer clear of these issues, you must be aware of them and avoid them as they come along.

Tempting Opportunities and Resources

As you start hanging on the internet, you will be meeting a lot of opportunities along with remarkable resources to promising you great support in your online business. These products, usually software or a business opportunity, may be as great as their vendor advertise them. Nonetheless, if you jump from one opportunity to another, you will be losing your focus on your core business. It is, therefore, important that you start an online business with only what you absolutely need and have it run smoothly before getting into another. The same works with your software or any other tool.

Neglecting New Opportunities

Basically, this is the exact opposite of grabbing every opportunity that comes along. If you refuse to examine or look at any new opportunity sent your way because you have your focus set up trying to achieve a goal with a method that simply don't work, avoid overlooking the warning signs that tell you that you need to move on or move in another direction.

Doing Everything by Yourself

When you think it's better to keep all the profit, you keep trying to do everything so you can keep the money to yourself. Saving is always good for your business, but as your business develops, it will become impossible for you to embrace all the tasks. This is the time when you need to develop some way to ease up your workload. An example of these if subscribing for an auto responder that will take care of your mailing activities. Instead of manually sending letters, answering queries, the auto-responder allows you to maintain and develop relationships with your customer base and up-sell or cross-sell your products and services.

Having Too Many Choices

Affiliate marketing is a good start for an online business for you can earn as soon as someone buys from your inks. This is the reason why it is so popular with many people. Affiliate marketing method has many positive aspects but there are too many choices that it is confusing to know which to promote. Before you jump into marketing a new software by way of an affiliate program, check how much commission you can earn from it, how you can get paid, and know if there is some support you can get from the owner. It is also important to know if the product sells before promoting it.

The Internet is Bigger than What You Think

Having an online business doesn't mean that people will naturally visit your website and buy things that you offer. The internet is such an enormous marketplace that you need to know how to get prospective customers to visit your visit so you can have the chance to convert these visits into sales. Meaning, you need to learn how to generate website traffic by utilizing both free and paid traffic generators.

No Support from Family and Friend

Sometimes, we presume that our family and friends will be our loyal customer. Sad to say, in most cases, it doesn't usually happen especially during the start of your business. There are even cases when they will discourage you from doing online business. Though these people mean well, don't get easily swayed and let your goals and efforts get destructed. If you have set your goal and created a business plan to back it up, you have every opportunity to get successful.

Regardless of whom you are, your age, gender, technical skills, educational background, you can always start your own internet business. You can always harness whatever skill you have through various learning platforms and resources provided on the internet for a certain fee or for free.

Download <u>Automatic Income Machines</u> NOW!

www.ingramcontent.com/pod-product-compliance
Lightning Source LLC
Chambersburg PA
CBHW081315180526
45170CB00007B/2723